dirty talk

dirty talk

SPEAK THE LANGUAGE OF LUST

by **Lynne Stanton**

ILLUSTRATIONS BY STAN CHOW

CHRONICLE BOOKS

SAN FRANCISCO

Library of Congress Cataloging-in-Publication Data available.
ISBN: 0-8118-5001-3

Manufactured in Hong Kong

Designed by **Jay Peter Salvas**
This book was typeset in Agendy 9/12, Bodoni Egyptian 9.5/14, Dalliance, Happy Hour, and Bickham Script

Distributed in Canada by Raincoast Books
9050 Shaughnessy Street
Vancouver, British Columbia V6P 6E5

10 9 8 7 6 5 4 3 2 1

Chronicle Books LLC
85 Second Street
San Francisco, California 94105

www.chroniclebooks.com

contents

Introduction   6

Section I : Finding Your Voice   13

Section II : Sharing the Love   43

Section III : Ramp It Up   71

In Closing . . .   118

Author Biography   120

introduction

Now, now, don't play so innocent.
You're not fooling anyone.
You know you've wanted to try it!

Sure, you're a nice girl, but there's no denying you've got a naughty side. Maybe you've even practiced what to say. Maybe you've gotten *this close* to actually whispering the words in your lover's ear. But somehow, in the heat of the moment, you find yourself tongue-tied. The words sound too embarrassing in your head. How could you possibly say these things out loud? Will he like it, you might wonder, or will he just think you're slutty? Or, worse yet, will he laugh? You find it's much safer to just moan. Murmuring "Oh my God" is as dirty as you get.

Meanwhile, everyone — from televised "sexperts" to mainstream women's magazines—advises you to try it. Let yourself go, they say. It's a turn-on for both of you, they swear. It's empowering and sexy and fun. You

believe them. But no one tells you exactly what to say or how to say it. Where's a girl to start?

Well, first things first: dirty talk is good for you. (Say it with me, girls!) It's true! There's no reason to be shy about something that's so positively beneficial. You see, besides turning you on, turning your partner on, and culminating in some much steamier sex (which everyone knows is good for everything from your complexion to your positive attitude to your cardiovascular health), dirty talk has a very important bonus. It's a terrific way for you to ask for — and get — exactly what you want in bed.

Chances are that you're the kind of woman who knows what she wants — from your dream job to that perfect pair of boots — and you have some idea of how to get it. Why should your sex life be any different? From encouragement ("Harder" and "Don't stop") to erotically charged instruction ("I get so hot when you kiss the

backs of my knees" and "Do it to me the way you did at that hotel in Memphis") to bringing secret fantasies vividly to life ("Oh my, I wasn't expecting the electrician today... Why, yes, the bedroom is right this way..."), you stand to get a whole lot more of what you want — if you just get used to talking about it. It's true, ladies: not only is dirty talk hot, but it's extremely useful, too.

Dirty talk also gives you the chance to discover brand new turn-ons not only for you but for your partner, too— whether he's a committed long-term love or a randy summer fling. Once you start talking to each other, you might unearth hot spots you didn't even know you had. Do you get all aquiver when he quotes lines from vintage erotica or the *Kama Sutra*? Does a whispered "Penthouse Forum" letter bring him to his knees? Or are you surprised to discover it's the other way around? You might be amazed at the words that are sexiest to each of you, once you start exploring them. And all of this will be your own little secret. How naughty! What fun!

Now, don't worry, none of this tawdry chat means you're cheap. Remember, you can talk a blue streak in the bedroom and still be a lady in the bright light of day. Accept this fact now, or you'll never be able to relax when the time comes to unveil your racy repertoire! In fact, one of the best-kept secrets of dirty talk is that you don't have to use a single dirty word, if you don't want to. You can describe a wild fantasy scene, a past encounter, an erotic dream, the particular acts you were thinking about when he was out of town, all in a suggestive and tantalizing way—in other words, good and naughty but with nary a naughty word. You'll see how. (Of course, if the forbidden four-letter words are the ones that fire you up most, by all means, use them!) Then again, there are moments when a well-timed "oh please" and your lover's name can be the dirtiest, and most effective, words around.

So, are you ready to start speaking the language of lust? This book will take you through it from start to finish.

Begin with tips to tackle your stage fright and ways to build your erotic vocabulary in "Finding Your Voice." Get ready to start dirty talking à deux in "Sharing the Love." Then, take your talk to the next level in "Ramp It Up" by using our role-play ideas and suggestions for practicing your new erotic lingo outside the boudoir.

let's
dive in!

finding your Voice

Don't worry; we're going to ease you into this—and, at least for now, no one needs to know. Learning how to dirty talk can be your own little secret, and like most secrets (especially if they're juicy), keeping your naughty lessons under wraps has its own benefit: it will give you an added dose of sexy mystery that simply wasn't there before. You might well find a new sashay in your step, a new boldness to your cocktail party banter, a new desire to show off that daring halter top. Yes, what you're working on alone in the evenings will stay with you all day long — how could it not? You will be practicing a very sensual art, and that will naturally give you a very sensual vibe, right from the start. You'll be charging your erotic batteries, and other people will feel that electricity — even before you say a word.

All that said, however, you still need to practice a little discipline if you're going to learn to dirty talk with the best of them. Dirty talking is intimate, fun, and freeing — but in order to discover all of that, you have to do it! And you simply won't do it if you don't practice. Just like learning piano, French, or how to downward dog, you can't reap the rewards if you never show up to class. So don't just flip through this book and say, "someday." Start tonight, on your own. Try the exercises that follow, and then repeat them. Get comfortable with speaking this new language so you can really do it with finesse! (And believe me, conjugating those verbs in Madame LeFleur's class was never this satisfying, *n'est pas?*)

Spit It Out

There's no way around it—you won't know what to say until you know what words turn you on. So you just have to spit some out. Words, I mean.

The best way to ease into dirty talking with a partner is to talk dirty alone. As silly as it sounds, you've got to start by saying some naughty words when you're by yourself—when you're driving, soaking in the tub, trying on a new outfit, or hiding under the covers. Get used to them. Take ownership of them. It may be really weird at first. But the more you say them now, the less you'll stumble over them later. In this way, rehearsing your smutty dialogue is no different than practicing a breakup speech or the keynote address at your high school reunion. Having a hard time choosing the words?

Start with some simple phrases:

> **Do you want me?**
>
> **Do you want to touch me there?**
>
> **Do you want to be inside me?**

Do you like that?

I want you.

I'm so horny.

I'm feeling naughty.

Take me, baby.

Do it now!

Harder, faster, deeper . . .

Yes, yes, yes!

You are so good.

I love it when you do _____.

you are so

big

Try all of these phrases multiple times, so you can get used to hearing yourself say them. Then, once you've covered the basics, expand your vocabulary a little. Get creative. Use your imagination. Think of a phrase a former lover might have said to you. Imagine what one of your fantasy partners would say if he came to life. Does talk of a spanking get you secretly revved up? Do you love the idea of doing it in a public place? Say words that fit in with these scenarios: "I've been bad!" or "But someone might see us!" Work out a short verbal script showing how things might progress from there. If you're still a bit stuck, you can turn to some

"I've been bad"

outside sources, like a smutty movie or book (see pages 32 and 36). Say what the characters say, even if you're not sure that you find their words sexy. Trust me, you won't know until you try them out loud.

"But someone might see us!"

After you hit upon a couple of favorite key words and phrases that you think might work for you, try them out loud again, when you're, you know, *flying solo*. Even something simple and easy, like "slower" and "faster" and "I like that" and "oh, yes", will help you get used to the sound of your own voice in an erotic context. Say these things over and over and over again. Test drive the dirty words for your

body parts (and his) to see which ones give you a thrill when you hear them. Try out different tones, different accents, different decibel levels. Try breathy and try demanding. Try innocent and try naughty. Try it while looking in the mirror and try it while hiding in a dark room. It's OK if you find the sound of the words distracting or embarrassing at first. You have to start somewhere! Remember there are no rules, so say anything you want, and see what works. You might find that embracing truly taboo words is surprisingly sexy to you, or that pretending you're a sweet innocent being seduced in her bed works even better. Just keep talking.

"oh, yes"

Build Your Erotic Vocabulary

Remember, things that might seem goofy, embarrassing, or trite in the light of day might seem totally hot during fore-play or orgasm. If you've run through the gamut of naughty words for body parts and exclamations like "oh, yes" and still found yourself tongue-tied during the act of love, it's time to call for backup. Luckily, there are plenty of ways to test out your erotic talk and decide what works for you—and plenty of places to steal good dialogue to use later.

Orgasm

TWO THUMBS UP!

One place to find inspiration is that old standby, porn. Unfortunately, most video porn doesn't include many actual words. After all, no one ever talks about the brilliant dialogue in *Deep Throat* or *Debbie Does Dallas*. While you might find only a few snippets of hot dialogue to work into your repertoire, what porn *can* offer in spades is a smorgasbord of naughty scenes and situations to steal and use, both in your mind *and* in your talk. This way, instead of garden-variety dirty declarations, you'll be able to describe a favorite movie turn-on scene of yours or your partner's. It's a perfect way to segue into dirty talk, because it allows you to be a bit removed, like a narrator of a play or a sportscaster. You'll simply be describing other people doing naughty things, so you can tell yourself it's not really coming from you. You get to be the voyeur. It's a great way to start.

Besides true porn, you can also check out R- and NC-17-rated movies with good sex scenes. Think about what got you hot and bothered at the movie theater in years past, poll your girlfriends, and even ask for recommendations at your video store if you're brave enough. (You can always tell them you're a graduate student doing a paper on nonexplicit erotica in American cinema.) Choose at least two or three movies to bring home, and plan to rack up some late charges. Pour yourself a big glass of wine, find your favorite scene, and watch it again and again. What do the characters say in the heat of the moment? What about the scene really gets you going? What would you change, if it were your own private fantasy?

When the hottest scene is over, hit pause and try to describe it out loud to yourself, including all the racy details. You can close your eyes if it helps, but try to be as specific as you can—really paint the scene. Once you've mastered the voice-over, dig deeper. Go through the suggested movie list (page 32) and find some more favorite scenes. Then, do your talking exercise again, but this time use the scene as just a springboard to dirty talk, and let yourself embellish— because the best dirty talk is customized to you. Rather than describing things verbatim, change it up. For example, if you found yourself turned on by the *Risky Business* train scene, you might put yourself in the scene and say, "The train is nearly empty, but not quite. It's late. I'm wearing only a slip dress and high heels, with nothing underneath. When I reach over to you, I see how hard you already are. You are looking at me like you can't wait to hike up my dress. Your

I SEE HOW **HARD** YOU ALREADY ARE!

hand is on my bare thigh. But we're not alone in the train car. You say, 'We can't.' I say, 'Yes, we can. We have to.' I can see another passenger in a dark overcoat, watching us intently. You brush my nipples with the back of your hand. The train rocks forward." Take it step by step, whispering so softly that you're barely audible if you need to. You're still doing it. You're talking dirty. And it's hot!

Enjoy describing these scenes on your own, practicing until you feel comfortable. Then, once you have a couple of hot scenarios burned into your mind, you'll have them at the ready whenever you want to bring them out, whether alone or with your partner (more on that later!).

Keep in mind that these movie scenes are just a starting place. Soon, you will no doubt find yourself using your erotic imagination to vary the scene and the dialogue, customizing it entirely to feature your own hot spots and favorite

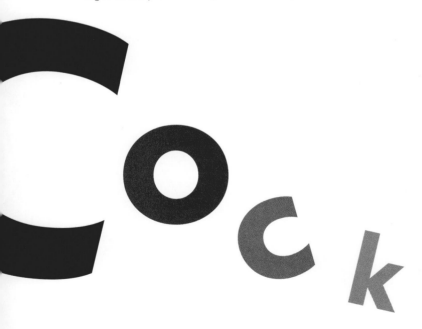

twists. Does he have a secret thing for airplane cockpits? Then try transporting the dirty-minded teenage boy and the high-class call girl of *Risky Business* to ten thousand feet up. Do you find the fantasy of a threesome unbelievably hot? Next time, have the passenger who was watching you on the train join you. You get the idea. What you'll end up with, after a few good tries, are brand-new fantasies that only the two of you know about, which are all the more sexually charged because of their secrecy. The possibilities are endless.

p i t

Movie Picks

Too shy to ask your neighborhood video clerk about porn?
Here are a handful of suggestions:

- *The Devil in Miss Jones*
- *Behind the Green Door*
- *Conquest*
- *Marie and Jack: A Hardcore Love Story*
- *The Masseuse*
- *Taken*
- *Bobby Sox*
- *Eyes of Desire*
- Anything by director Candida Royale (one of the
  few females in the biz)

If traditional porn leaves you cold, try mainstream movies
with hot seduction scenes—and remember that it doesn't
have to be a great movie, it just needs a great sex scene
that you can fast-forward to.

- *Belle de Jour*

- *The Big Easy*

- *Body Heat*

- *Basic Instinct*

- *Bound*

- *Henry & June*

- *The Lover*

- *9½ Weeks*

- *The Unbearable Lightness of Being*

- *The English Patient*

- *Dangerous Liaisons*

- *An Affair of Love / Une Liaison Pornographique*

- *Sex and Lucía*

- *Sirens*

And there's always *Risky Business* and that really hot train scene with a young Tom Cruise and Rebecca De Mornay.

BECOME A NAUGHTY LIBRARIAN

This brings us to our next source for cribbing naughty language and making it your own: erotic literature. Please think of the term "literature" very, very loosely. You don't have to go highbrow—dirty magazines, pulp novels, contemporary short stories, and online confessional essays all count. Hey, if it's written down and it turns you on, it's erotic literature.

As you're building your bedroom lingo, make it a point to keep naughty books and magazines at your bedside. Become well read in all forms of smut, and you'll become well versed in dirty talk. You never know what words and phrases from your late-night reading will find their way to your lips in the heat of the moment. Try reading everything from trashy novels from the fifties to current porn magazines to serious erotica. What scenes and phrases turn you on the most? What shocks you a little? What do you think is way too dirty to ever say out loud? Highlight some favorite passages, from all different genres. Now, lock your door and read your selections aloud. Slowly.

Again and again.

Check It Out

Never dipped into naughty bedside reading? Here are a few places to start.

- ∞ Anything by Anaís Nin: try *Delta of Venus, Little Birds,* or *A Journal of Love*

- ∞ Anything by Henry Miller

- ∞ Anything by Nancy Friday: try *My Secret Garden, Forbidden Flowers,* or *Women on Top*

- ∞ *Fear of Flying* by Erica Jong

- ∞ *The Story of O* by Pauline Reage: a classic erotic novel

- ∞ *Sweet Life: Erotic Fantasies for Couples* by Violet Blue

- ∞ *The Best American Erotica* and other anthologies

- ∞ *Penthouse, Playboy,* and other skin mags (You've got to give 'em a shot, just to see what the fuss is about.)

- ∞ Classic pulp fiction, Victorian bodice-rippers, and Gothic novels (Scour your local bookstore for some dog-eared favorites with racy covers.)

With books, as with movies, you'll likely find it's easier to start your dirty-talking career with other people's words. That way, if you decide it sounds ridiculous, it's someone else's fault! Just as you did with the movies, find a section—a paragraph, passage, or even a whole chapter—that gets you going, and do your first readings straight from the page. After trying that, go further. Adjust the words or situations a bit to make them even hotter to you. You can turn a girl character into a boy, change a bit of dialogue, or add a dirty twist—go ahead, try it! Read it aloud again with your improvements, and note them for next time. Another exercise is to rewrite your favorite passages completely, jotting your new and improved scene down in a bedside journal.

DO IT GU
WITH

Once your naughty book or magazine has given you some erotic inspiration, feel free to take on the role of author and change the cast of characters (or the number of characters!), the time of day, or even the period of history (why can't a steamy sixties club scene be transported to a medieval castle, if you like that better?). Read your new version out loud, making sure there's plenty of steamy dialogue.

See how good the words sound out loud? Don't you think your partner would *die* to hear your dramatic reading — especially between the sheets? It might be time to share your new vocabulary with him. Don't be shy — practice makes perfect, and by this time, you've practiced plenty! When you're ready to bring in your captive audience, read on for ideas on *sharing the love.*

JSTO

Call Girl

What better way to learn to talk dirty than to listen to a pro do it live? No, you don't have to hire a hooker. You can get a lesson in the privacy of your own bedroom by calling a phone sex line. No one ever has to know! If you're willing to fork over some dough, turn to those tawdry pages at the back of the local free or alternative newspaper, or look online, and just choose one—making sure it's a live chat, not a recording.

Try talking to men, to women, to couples, until you find some dirty talk that works for you. Don't forget to take notes, if you're not too busy getting turned on.

Sharing the

Love

Hopefully, your solo erotic life has improved immensely since you began this book. Perhaps you've even called in sick so you could spend the day in bed with your stack of erotica! And no doubt, if you have a man in your life, he's been reaping the rewards of your humming libido as well, even if you're still too shy to tell him exactly what you've been up to. Well, it only gets better from here—

because it's time to bring your partner in on the fun, in a big way. There's no need to hold back. Let me tell you, there's not a man alive who's not titillated by the idea of a woman whispering sweet nothings to him that are, well, not sweet at all.

Ease yourself in, if you're not sure how he'll react — or if you're ready. Begin by using sexier language in your e-mails and text messages, and see what kind of response you get. Be extra saucy during a late-night phone call. Try introducing him to those movies you find hot, and watch your favorite scenes together, so you'll have a shared vocabulary that you can whisper about later. Loan him one of the erotic books you loved. While you're in bed, ask him to describe an erotic scene from his youth, or share one with him. There are so many tantalizing ways to get started talking dirty *à deux*! In the pages that follow, you'll find suggestions to get things rolling.

Read It

Sometimes this is the easiest place to start — rather than using your own made-up words, you and your beau can share someone else's. Start by leaving a stack of your erotic discoveries on his side of the bed, after flagging your favorite passages. You might want to leave them for him to peruse (with a tarty note attached) when you're out with the girls, and then jump into bed and talk about his favorites when you come home. Don't forget to ask him what kind of reading *he* finds hot, and then pick up some of his preferred literature to add to your stack of goodies—even if it's *Playboy* or *Barely Legal*. Ask him to put into words what turns him on about those magazines, and then tell him what you find hot about your own choices. Opening up about this is all excellent practice in the art of erotic talk. When you take turns reading each other's hot stuff, it will only help you know what to say to each other when the time comes.

Take it to the next level by planning a night where you head to bed (or the tub) early together, and read your erotica or porn in tandem. It's so much better than another rerun of *Friends*! You can each read silently on your own, sharing the passages that you find particularly steamy, or read aloud. If you've never done this before, you'll find that it's such a treat: closing your eyes and hearing your man read naughty bits to you will be a revelation—for you and for him.

After you've done this a few times, you might choose to customize a particular story in a way that you think your partner might like better—just as you tried on your own. Change locations, the ages of the characters, and what they do. Include sexy pet names or places and situations that are erotically charged for the two of you. Embellish, bringing in your own erotic histories and fantasies to make the stories juicier. Soon, you'll know what's working and you'll no longer need the books to help you weave an erotic tale. Plus, realizing how steamy it is to hear each other's voices say these things will only inspire you to talk dirty more often!

Write It

Dirty writing isn't exactly the same as dirty talking, but it's close. Both require the guts to go out on a limb and share with one another the words and phrases that you find sexy, and both give you the opportunity to discover your mate's turn-ons. We've all probably written a racy e-mail or letter at some point in the past, and if we're lucky we've received a good one, too. Just thinking about it might give you butter-flies—oh, the things he said! Something about seeing those naughty and forbidden words in a lover's handwriting—and being able to hold on to them to read again and again—is truly hot. So why don't we all do this more often? This week, set aside some time to write a naughty letter to your man, even if you live with him. Put it somewhere unex-pected, like inside the refrigerator, behind his neckties, or under the windshield wiper of his car. (It's even

start a
steamy
correspondence

better if you can mail it to him at the office — clearly marking it "personal" on the envelope!) In the letter, describe what you'd like him to do to you the next time you're together, or write about a move or position that brought you to your knees the last time. Make sure you ask for a reply, starting a steamy correspondence. (By the way, *Dangerous Liaisons* has a great scene where John Malkovich writes a love letter on Uma Thurman's bottom; you may want to try this technique at home!)

Besides formal letters, all kinds of writing can ease you into using words as erotic tools. Try an exercise where each of you writes down one sexual fantasy and then shares it— aloud if you dare. Or, write several simple sexual fantasies on slips of paper and put them into a hat, and then take turns drawing a fantasy and reading it aloud—which may even lead to acting it out. A naughty note left in the brief-case is an oldie but a goodie; briefly describe a previous romp, an erotic dream, or a very specific act you plan to do later. Send a text message or e-mail (using your *personal* accounts!) with an innocuous-sounding header but a truly racy message. (At work, you can even get away with using code words from your shared erotic vocabulary in your e-mails. You could just type the words "Remember the train?" or sign your message "Your French schoolgirl," and you'll set his heart racing — he'll know *exactly* what you mean.) Later, whisper your favorite excerpts of your lover's letter into his ear, or have him read his letter aloud to you.

Watch It

Remember your solo movie exercise? Now it's time to unleash those lessons you learned on your partner. If you're feeling shy, start by watching that favorite flick alone, maybe when your man is out of town, and then call and try describing it to him—in delicious detail, of course. Begin the conversation normally: "Hey honey, you know what I rented tonight? *The Lover*. Have you ever seen it? Well, there's this one really hot scene. It's late afternoon and this French schoolgirl is on her way home. She has her hair in braids and she's wearing one of those little plaid skirts. But waiting for her outside the school is a car, with a man inside. She gets into the backseat . . ." Keep going

from there, and make it as naughty as you dare. Gauge his reaction (and be prepared for him to show up at your door before the closing credits!) and then next time, try it in person. During your next quiet date night at home, take a pause in your make-out session to dive in to a dirty description as things heat up between you two. Start describing one of *your* scenes. It doesn't matter if he's seen the movie or not. Just lean into him on the couch and whisper, "Close your eyes and picture this. You're waiting for me in the car and I climb into the back-seat. I'm wearing one of those short little plaid skirts . . ." Slowly set up the characters for him, the smells, the buildup, what everyone is wearing. Include as many tarty adjectives as you can.

silky

soft

wet

hard

moist

slippery

hot

steamy

secret

forbidden

Walk him through it. He may be surprised at first, but chances are he'll quickly catch on to what you're doing—and you'll know it by his response. He might even join in the talk, taking it to a new place. Go with it. As the two of you get hotter, so should the scene you're describing. Let the urgency creep into your voice, and into the scene. By the time you get to the main course, you'll both be transported to that place and time—and it's much, much easier to talk dirty when you're somewhere other than your living room on a Tuesday night.

Remember It

Your best springboard for dirty talk with your partner is right at your fingertips: your own sex life. Instead of using fantasy scenes, try talking about what you've already done together—you'll be amazed at how sexy that is! During foreplay, as things heat up, slowly start reminiscing about that really hot time: "Oh my God, do you remember how we disappeared at your parents' house last Thanksgiving, and you took me upstairs? Remember? We had to be quick so we didn't even get undressed. You just unzipped your pants and . . ." I guarantee it, hearing you describe it (and hearing you say that you want him again, in the same way) will be a massive turn-on.

Imagine It

This is a great exercise in your dirty-talk career. Try this: you and your partner, during foreplay, simply share erotic stories, narrating to each other. You can use one of your fantasy scenes from your book or movie research, or just start with a very simple premise: you've walked in on someone having sex at a party, you can see into someone else's apartment, or you're sitting topless by the pool when the new gardener happens by. One of you can choose to be the sole narrator, allowing the other person to just visualize the scene, or you can take turns—you start out with a sentence, then he picks up the story, then you. This dirty little game has the added benefit of building upon itself— over time, you'll have a whole repertoire of fantasies that you can go to in an instant.

Ask for It

Remember, one of the best ways to talk dirty is to ask for what you want. Rather than grunting and moaning and hoping he'll interpret these sounds correctly, just tell it like it is! You can do this in a very sexy way. Simple instructions ("slower," "faster," "harder," "to the left," "to the right") coupled with very vocal praise when he does what you ask ("Oh, yes! Oh God, that's the spot, right there!") is a no-brainer and probably comes naturally to you already. But as you get used to talking dirty with each other, you'll get more comfortable being *very* specific. If you usually let him initiate things, ask him for *exactly* what you want tonight: for him to go down on you, do it from behind, tie you up, blindfold you, or tease you mercilessly until you say the magic word. If you want a particular act or position, tell him what it is and how much you want it that way. If you crave more foreplay, whisper to him what you want him to do, and how hot it makes you when he takes it slow and does those things. (You both might also find that talking him all the way through it is really sexy: "Now, you're gently running your tongue just along the edge of my panties, but no farther . . .") Or, if you want it fast and hard tonight, let him know—by demanding it, or by begging him for it. Either way, he'll love it! And, God knows, so will you.

Hear It

Part of being a good dirty talker is being a good dirty listener. Pay attention to what works for your partner, and what he says in return. Think about his choices in erotic books and movies, his favorite notes and letters from you, and where he takes the fantasy talk. When you start talking dirty, what makes him breathe faster? What makes him moan? What makes him hard? Pay attention, and store this information away for next time. (Be sure to give him *your* clues in return, by responding clearly to what works for you, and telling him, too—"Wow, last night when we started talking about that time at your parents', I found that so hot.") Soon, you'll grow to know just what your partner likes to hear, which will only boost your dirty talk confidence—and fun.

Phone Home

If you and your man haven't ever shared an erotic phone call, it's an essential step in your dirty-talk education. The reason is simple: the phone forces you to talk. You can't use anything but your voice—no hands, no tongues, no facial expressions.

While this may seem intimidating to the novice dirty talker, remember, the phone does impose a kind of anonymity if you feel a bit shy. You may find it's much easier to talk dirty on the phone, because you're all alone, with no one looking at you. Set a time when you both feel comfortable, have at least a half hour to kill, and won't be interrupted— maybe when you're each at your own apartment across town late at night, or when one of you is on a business trip or working late. Take your time. Talk about what you would do if you were together, or reminisce about a previous encounter. Or, bring out one of your favorite fantasies and take it up a notch, making it even racier by trying out dirty words that may surprise him. (Remember, you don't even have to be you. Anything is fair game on the phone.) Now, one thing may lead to another, and you might find yourself segueing from a naughty conversation to actual phone sex. If so, don't worry about results; just enjoy the moment. Describe what you're doing, ask him to describe what he's doing, and then discuss what you wish your partner could do if he were there in person. Try asking for things that you might be hesitant to ask for if you were together. Try being yourselves, or try being completely different people. Talk all the way.

What Not to Say

OK, so you've learned a lot about what you and your partner like to hear. But let's talk about what can kill the mood—fast.

Keep your mouth shut about . . .

- *Household minutiae.* Yes, you may suddenly remember, in the middle of foreplay, an overdue bill or something you need at the store. There's no reason he needs to know this.

- *Your period.* If you happen to have a man who understands your cycle, good for you. But still.

- *Your digestion, or other nonerotic bodily processes.* Tonight's shrimp didn't agree with you? Take a break from the action if you need to, but don't talk about it in the heat of the moment.

- *Your pets.* Yes, you can both hear Fifi scratching to get in. Ignore her. She's a dog—she'll be OK for the next seventeen minutes.

- *The time.* Running late? Let it go. Don't ever ask what time it is or express concern about the hour—unless you can do it in an erotic way ("Do it to me quick, baby— someone might come in!").

- *References to anyone's mother or father.* 'Nuff said.

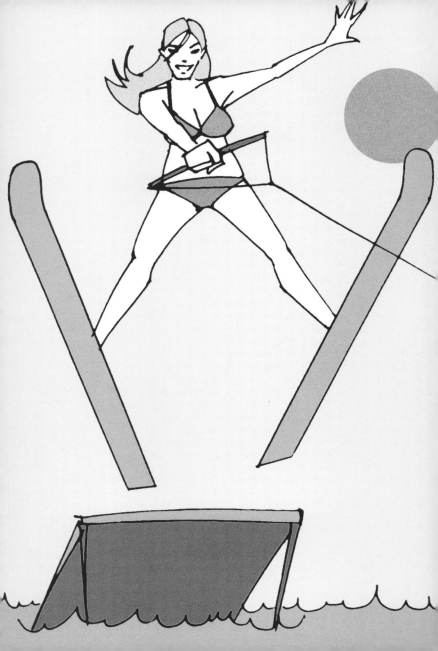

Ramp It Up

Congratulations—you've mastered the basics! By now, you've eased into saying naughty things, alone and with your partner. You've got a hot vocabulary in place, and you know what particular words, phrases, and spoken scenarios make your heart (and his) beat faster. Hopefully, the two of you have developed a very sexy rhythm and rapport—and you've found that you can slip into your racy dialogue as easily as your favorite lingerie. You know how to use outside sources to get you hot, how to mine your own sexual histories, how to play games together, and how to ask for what you want. Now you're ready to take it further. This is where things get *really* naughty!

Now that you're comfortable talking dirty as *yourself*, it's time to take it up a notch by being someone else. Talk about a turn-on—you can try on different personas that you and your partner find enticing, you can be someone very naughty or very nice, and both you and your man get the thrill of experiencing someone wildly different while making love only with each other. It's playing around without playing around. Think about it: you can finally have a one-night stand with a sexy stranger and not regret it in the morning!

Think you don't have it in you to role-play? Oh, come on! Here are a few ideas to pique your imagination and get you over your initial stage fright. Remember, for these memorable nights in the privacy of your own home, you can be any character you want. Picture the sexiest twosome you can think of (say, a delicious young stewardess in a short skirt and a dashing pilot in uniform), put them in any lusty situation (her sitting on his lap in the cockpit and trying out the controls, when she feels his hand move up her bare thigh), talk it through together (enjoying the twists and turns the stories take when you say them aloud), and then just do it—as *them*. Try out a few scenarios until you find your favorites—and his—and then bring them out whenever you feel like mixing things up in the bedroom.

fantasy
fantasy
FANTASY
Fantasy

Be Whatever You Desire

Don't just settle for what you think he might find sexy, or what society might find sexy—play around until you discover what personas and qualities make *you* feel the most sexy. Remember, anything goes! Through dirty talk and a little imagination, you can be sweet and innocent tonight, and a dominatrix tomorrow.

You Can Be Exotic

Always wish you were an international girl of mystery? Learn a few key words or phrases in another language, particularly a romantic one like Spanish, Italian, or French. Your words will sound terribly exotic, the foreign tongue will take you out of yourself, and everything will likely be less embarrassing for you to say. After all, many people find a whispered *"baisez-moi"* even sexier to hear, and to say, than *"fuck me,"* oui?

∞ *"Hágalo a mí duramente."* (Spanish for "Do it to me hard.")

∞ *"Lei è cosi grande!"* (Italian for "You are so big!")

∞ *"Tome-me a cama imediatamente."* (Portuguese for "Take me to bed immediately!")

∞ *"Dieu, je suis si movillé et excité."* (French for "My God, I am so wet and horny.")

∞ Or just pepper your good ol' English sexy talk with some key exotic words: tell him that you find him unbelievably *caliente* ("hot" in Spanish), *grande* ("big" in French), *atractivo* ("sexy" in Spanish), or *duro come una roccia* ("hard as a rock" in Italian).

YOU CAN BE BOSSY

Usually let him call the shots? You're not alone. But imagine how surprised—and horny—he'll be when you demand sex with him, telling him you can't wait another second. It's every man's fantasy.

➳ **"Do it to me, baby. Do it!"**

➳ **"Make me come."**

∞ "Take me hard," "Give it to me," or "Go down on me."

∞ "Tie me down."

∞ "Deeper, deeper, faster, faster, don't stop."

YOU CAN BE INNOCENT

Men love to imagine themselves in charge now and then, as the seducer of a sweet young thing—even if you've been together for years. Play to his secret deflowering fantasies.

∓ "I promise to be good."

∓ "I'll do anything you want."

∓ "Spank me. I've been very bad."

∓ "May I touch it?"

∓ "Ooh, it's so big!"

∓ "Please be gentle with me. I've never done this before."

YOU CAN LAVISH HIM WITH PRAISE

Everyone likes to be stroked — especially in the bedroom.
If you make him feel like the greatest lover in the world,
your compliments will no doubt be paid back in full. Watch
and see.

∞ "You're the king."

∞ "You are so hot."

∞ "You get me so hot."

∞ "You're gorgeous/sexy/amazing/an unbelievable lover."

∞ "You are the best fuck I've ever had."

∞ "All my friends want you."

∞ "You drive me absolutely wild."

∞ "Where did you learn how to do that?"

∞ "You are the master."

YOU CAN BE MEAN

It may not be to everyone's taste, but some folks enjoy being chastised and punished a little. In an intimate moment, tease your man by asking if he wants a spanking or other forms of "domination lite." If he seems intrigued, try it out. You might *both* like it!

∞ "You've been very bad."

∞ "Shame on you!"

∞ "Get down on your knees."

∞ "It's time for your punishment."

∞ "No, you can't touch me. I won't let you."

∞ "You don't deserve it."

∞ "Are you ready to work for it?"

∞ "You have to earn it!"

⚙ YOU CAN EXAGGERATE

Now, there's nothing wrong with a little embellishment—
or even a white lie—to keep things hot and heavy in the
bedroom. Perhaps in your regular life you're a no-nonsense
straight shooter. Throw that away tonight, and be the girl
who makes him feel like he's king of the world.

∞ "You are so huge. You're almost too big!"

∞ "You are the biggest/hottest/sexiest man I've
    ever known."

∞ "You can go all night, can't you, big boy?"

∞ "Every time I touch myself, I think of you."

∞ "No one's ever fucked me like you do."

∞ "You have the most amazing cock in the world."

∞ "You're the best I've ever had."

YOU CAN TELL HIM WHAT YOU WANT

As you learned earlier, dirty talk can also help you direct your man to do exactly what you desire. In the heat of the moment, don't expect him to read your mind—tell him where to go and what to do! (And if he's doing it right, keep the positive encouragement coming!)

∞ "That's it; right there, stay right there."

∞ "Do it like you did it last time."

∞ "Slower."

∞ "Faster."

∞ "To the right."

∞ "To the left."

∞ "Tease me."

∞ "Hold me down."

∞ "Tie me up."

∞ "Go down on me."

∞ "Take me from behind."

∞ "Get on top of me."

∞ "Let me get on top of you."

∞ "Get inside me right now!"

YOU CAN USE DIRTY WORDS

OK, maybe you've found your favorite sexy words—but have you tried the really, truly filthy words? Hey, don't knock foul language until you've tried it. Even if you think you won't find it hot, you might be surprised—hearing yourself, or your lover, use forbidden and four-letter terms in the middle of some steamy sex can be both freeing and exciting.

can whisper

can scream

can say yes

can say no

can use profanity

can tease

can give in

can be naughty

can be nice

And then, you can fantasize . . .

Welcome to Fantasy Island

Time for a change of scenery? Through the art of dirty talk, you can change not only your persona but your entire situation too. Be a sultry wench in a medieval castle, a French cancan girl in twenties Paris, a nubile student on holiday, a cheerleader getting a ride home from the coach after practice, a call girl on her first job, an older woman tutoring a young protégé, a naughty executive in a boardroom after hours, a lady of leisure eyeing the mansion's gardener. Any scene that has ever flitted through your mind in the heat of the moment is fair game! You'll find that talking about it aloud—and sharing it—makes the fantasy much more vivid, and therefore much hotter, than it ever was in your head.

By this point in the game, you and your partner are used to talking dirty and are ready to playact. It's delicious fun with a casual love interest, and it's a fantastic thrill with a long-term lover — you get to experiment with all sorts of sexy scenarios without leaving your own happy bedroom. Schedule a "fantasy night," if you want to get geared up— and not chicken out. Have some wine and watch a sexy movie, if that helps. Talk through your fantasies in the dark, under the covers, or even blindfolded, if you're self-conscious. Take turns if you like, encouraging each other to say what you really mean, and helping each other through the parts where you might stumble or giggle. Through talk, you two can explore things you find titillating as fantasies but might not want to try in real life—like group sex, threesomes, public sex, or S&M. If you trust your partner, this is a safe way to get close to those forbidden desires, without really doing them. And really go to town on the details—set the scene, the time of day, the cast of characters, what everyone is wearing. Make it as vivid as possible the first few times around; after a while, just a key phrase, like "Paris nightclub" or "swingers' party," will be enough to bring it instantly to life, like the most memorable scene of a favorite film.

Can't begin to imagine telling your lover that fantasy you have about doing it with a fireman on the bed of a speeding truck, much less the one about being felt up by two other girls at a strip club? If you like, ease in with some of the following fantasies before you divulge your own inner dreams. OK, so some of these scenarios are cliché. But there's a reason they're cliché—they work! Here are some "go to" fantasies to get you started talking.

FANTASY 101

Put on something saucy, get into bed with your man, have a nightcap, and talk about what happens when you are . . .

∞ Surprised by a delivery man when stepping out of the shower

∞ Awoken by a stranger while sleeping on the train

∞ Seduced by the pilot in an airplane cockpit

∞ Fondled under the table at a fancy dinner party by someone else's date

∞ Swimming with another couple in a secluded lake, when one thing leads to another

∞ Getting a massage from a beautiful masseur (or masseuse) when you feel hands going where they shouldn't

∞ Blindfolded and touched by a stranger, without knowing whether it's a man or a woman

∞ Accidentally witnessing another hot couple having sex through a window

∞ Asleep upstairs at a party, when a few amorous guests find their way into the room and start going at it

∞ Pulled over by a very persuasive and hot policeman on a dark, deserted road

∞ Bent over by the burly mechanic when you take your car in for service

∞ The center of attention at a swingers' party, with everyone watching as someone goes down on you

∞ Seduced by your new boss on the conference table after hours

blindf

olded

ROLE PLAY AS FOREPLAY

Perhaps, in all the fantasies mentioned, you are still you—
you've just dropped in to the fantasy scene. But remember,
not only can you be somewhere else, you can be some*one*
else. It's amazingly freeing to be another person for an hour
or so, saying all the things she would say and doing all the
things she might do, without repercussions or responsibil-
ity. You get a chance to slip into someone else's life, and
there's no doubt that lovemaking will be different as "her."
And after the hot romp is finished, you'll feel like you've
had a little vacation from your real life. And remember,
role-playing is even better together—encourage him to be
someone else, too, so you can both disappear into the
erotic scene.

If you need some help getting started, take on the persona
of someone in a dirty story or movie you've seen. Use
her name. Say what she would say, do what she would do.
See how it feels to have sex as her. What does she do dif-
ferently? What noises does she make? What does she do
to your partner that's different from what you usually do?
What does she say out loud that you would never, ever say
yourself? In doing this, you'll develop a persona you can
bring out once in a while, someone you both get a thrill from.

So whom do you want to be? And what on earth would
that person say, if she were talking dirty? When you get
ready to open your mouth in bed (to talk dirty, that is),
think about . . .

What would the **dirty nurse** say?

Maybe something like "OK now, it's time for your sponge bath. Please take everything off, and the candy striper and I will get started on you. Now, what's dirty? Oh my, that *is* dirty. Maybe we'll have to use some tongue on that. Would that be all right? Let me just close the curtain. Don't tell the doctor . . ."

What would the **naughty schoolgirl** say?

Maybe something like "I'm here for my French lesson, Monsieur X. If you don't tell my parents I'm failing, I'll work very, very hard—on whatever you like. Very hard. I really need an A. Can I sit on your lap while we work on our verbs? What's the French word for lap, again? What about the French word for tickle? Or spank? Say it again. Say it again. Oh la la! I've never done *this* before!"

What would the **hot executive** say?

Maybe something like "I know it's late, Mr. Smith, but we need to talk about your performance. I need you to be working much, much harder. How hard are you willing to work for me? I need to see more drive, more stamina. And I really need you to do everything I ask—otherwise, you know I can fire you. Let's start with a neck rub; I'm so tense. That's good. Mmmmm. Now maybe I'll unbutton my blouse a little bit. Remember, Mr. Smith, I'm the boss here, so let's see how you perform for me."

Now, you try.

What would the sexy **French maid** say?

What would the **voyeur** say?

What would the **porn star** say?

What would the **call girl** say?

What would the **promiscuous babysitter** say?

What would the **oversexed debutante** say?

What would the **stripper** say?

What would the **horny housewife** say?

Erotic Twosome Ideas

Use these role-play ideas to get the juices flowing.

- Stripper & customer
- Model & photographer
- Nurse or doctor & patient
- Hitchhiker & driver
- Student & teacher
- Pilot & stewardess
- Bank teller & robber
- Boss & employee
- Lord & wench
- Gangster & showgirl

- Neighbor & neighbor

- Kidnapper & hostage

- Bad boy & good girl

- Bad girl & good boy

- Prison warden & prisoner

- Lifeguard & bathing beauty

- Porn star & director

- Intruder & homeowner

- Virgin & seducer

- Hooker & client

- Gardener & lady of the house

- Chauffeur & passenger

- Police officer & criminal

- Cheerleader & football player

- Repairman & housewife

Take It Outside!

Great news—now that you've learned all this, you don't have to limit your dirty-talk expertise to the boudoir. In fact, you can have great fun trying it in wildly different places! You've mastered erotic lingo—so remember, there are other uses for it besides breathless words uttered in the heat of the moment. Make it a part of your life. Whether at a boring party, on the bus, or right before you walk into a restaurant for dinner, bring out those phrases that have sexy meaning to the two of you—and watch the sparks fly.

In fact, you might find that the blue talk you've practiced in the bedroom is even more effective if you *are* in a public place, where you can't immediately satisfy your urges. Trust me, if you quietly say something like "I can't wait to

have you inside me" while on a crowded airplane, it will make the flight—or at least the subsequent arrival—much steamier for both of you. Throw out a phrase like "Remember that time we were on the train, and I wasn't wearing any panties, and you took me hard right there?" mere moments before you walk into his stuffy office party, and you'll be in for a very interesting end to the evening. If you're feeling really dirty, who knows—your little chat might lead to some quick play in an upstairs bedroom or coat closet! And if not, once you're safely home you can always *pretend* that you had a quickie in the coat closet—talk about it! Try, "Oh God, someone might see us, your boss might walk in, we have to be quick, we have to be quiet, just lift up my dress, oh God, someone's coming!"

This week, try whispering a dirty phrase to your lover at least once when . . .

∞ He's walking out the door for work

∞ Your dinner guests are ringing your doorbell

∞ You're on your morning commute together

∞ He's on the phone with someone else

∞ You're at a crowded cocktail party

∞ You've just rolled over to go to sleep

∞ You're on the way into the shower

∞ He's doing a mundane chore, like dishes or laundry

∞ You're waiting for the bus

∞ You're on an airplane

∞ You're in the back of a taxi

∞ You're at a bar or restaurant

∞ He's about to go into a big meeting

∞ You have people over

∞ You're at someone else's house

BE NOTEWORTHY

Another way to bring dirty talk into your daily life is to pass it along even when you're not physically with your man. Erotic talk doesn't always have to be spoken. Get double duty out of all your favorite lingo by using those X-rated words, scenes, and dialogue in saucy e-mails (from your personal account, please!) or smutty letters and notes. This is equally effective with a long-term partner, someone you're dating casually, or even a hottie you haven't slept with yet. That's right—don't slack off just because you're temporarily single. Keep yourself in shape for when the time is right!

∞ Leave a smutty note in your man's pocket, tucked in his briefcase, or taped to the toilet seat.

∞ Tape an enticing note to your front door for him to find when he comes home—and finish the sentiment when he gets inside.

∞ Write a deliciously naughty fantasy in your bedside journal, and then either mail it to him or "accidentally" leave it lying about the bedroom where he'll find it.

∞ Scribble a smutty phrase in lipstick across his bathroom mirror—with a promise of what's to come later.

∞ Pack your man's lunch one day, with a decidedly unhousewifely note inside.

- ∞ Send a steamy, erotic, and specific letter to your man's apartment. If you live together, send it to his work (mark it "Confidential"!).

- ∞ Jot something dirty on a bar or restaurant napkin, and pass it to him before excusing yourself to go to the ladies' room.

- ∞ Pass him a sexy note while in a plane, train, or automobile (extra points if it includes an idea of something you can do right then and there).

Play Games

Dirty talk doesn't have to be serious business. Besides the overheated chatter that naturally arises between the sheets, you can play games to get the erotic talk flowing. Here are a few suggestions.

∞ Remember that game at camp, where one person says a sentence and the next person has to say the next? Do a dirty version. Start simply, with something like "The handsome stranger at the bar looked like he had a secret" or "The lifeguard noticed her sunbathing topless by the pool."

∞ Set your own dirty-talk rules for the evening. For example: "Tonight, I can say whatever I want; but you can say two words only: 'please' and 'baby.'" Hold him to it—and tease him mercilessly—by stopping the action if you hear even one utterance that's not on your list.

∞ Open a bottle of wine, and then have each of you make a list of sexy words and phrases. No peeking! Swap your lists, and take turns saying them out loud. Laughing is OK. Remember the favorites for later!

∞ Blindfold one of you, and then let the blindfolded person describe what he's "seeing" in his fantasy, while you help things along with touch.

Decide which one of you is tonight's dirty talker. Then tie a scarf around the other person's mouth. Let the talker lead the action.

Try naughty versions of standard games: play strip poker, strip Twister, dirty-word Scrabble (just use the real game, but only naughty words), dirty-minded truth-or-dare, or naked hide-and-seek.

in **closing**

Congratulations! You're well on your way to mastering the language of lust—and it only gets better from here, with more practice, less inhibition, and plenty of sexy discoveries along the way. Be sure to keep in tip-top talking shape by practicing your lines—and having lots of dress rehearsals, with or without an audience! Learning to talk naughty, and enjoying it, is an essential

part of your erotic education—those essential lessons you never learned in school but are so much more gratifying and useful than geometry or home ec. It's hot, it's fun, it's eye-opening, and—just like any new sexual act or position—it's a great chance to experiment with your desires and find out what gives you the most satisfaction. And what could be better than that?

Now you've learned it for yourself: dirty talk *is* good for you! Go forth and spread the word.

Lynne Stanton is a freelance writer who is almost never tongue-tied. She lives in Seattle with her husband and spends as much time as possible under the covers.

Stan Chow's illustrations have appeared on book covers and in numerous newspapers and magazines including *Elle*, *Cosmopolitan*, and *GQ*. He lives in Manchester, England.